A STAINED-GLASS WINDOW

Scriptures, Poems, and Short Stories

by

Jamael Robert McCauley

www.TrueVinePublishing.org

A Stained-Glass Window
Jamael Robert McCauley

Published by
True Vine Publishing Co.
810 Dominican Dr.
Nashville, TN 37228
www.TrueVinePublishing.org

NIV: New International Version

Scripture quotations taken from The Holy Bible, New International Version® NIV®

Copyright © 1973, 1978, 1984, 2011 by Biblica, Inc. Used with permission. All rights reserved worldwide.

ISBN: 978-1-968092-62-7 Paperback
ISBN: 978-1-968092-63-4 eBook

Printed in the United States—First printing

ACKNOWLEDGEMENTS

I would like to thank God for being the source of my strength, creativity, and hope. Every word in this book was written with His guidance and grace.

To my family and loved ones—thank you for your unwavering support, patience, and encouragement. Your belief in me made this journey possible.

To my friends, mentors, and teachers who listened, challenged me, and inspired me—your words and presence shaped these pages more than you know.

Finally, to every reader who finds themselves in these poems: Thank you for allowing my words to enter your world.

FOREWORD

It is a rare and profound privilege to introduce the work of a man whose voice I first encountered in the bustling newsroom of *The Meter* at Tennessee State University. Back then, Jamael Robert McCauley and I were young reporters and editors, fueled by the energy of North Nashville and the weight of telling our college stories. Today, as he stands on the threshold of 50, Jamael has transitioned from reporting the news to capturing the very soul of the human experience in this stunning collection, *A Stained-Glass Window*.

This book is a masterclass in the "uncommon". Jamael, now an educator molding the minds of eighth graders, has clearly never stopped being a student of the world around him. In these pages, he takes the grit of the streets—the "potholes," the "man down" calls, and the "displaced hate"—and refracts them through a lens of profound faith and redemption.

His poetry does not flinch. He speaks of the "malnutrition" of the soul in "Pumpkin" and the "generational genocide" that stalks our neighborhoods. Yet, like the stained-glass windows he admired as a child at Holy Rosary, he shows us that even the most "broken people" can create a "breathtaking" image when the light of grace shines through them.

As his former editor, I see the same tenacity I remember from our college days, but it is now tempered by a "fireside" wisdom that only comes with time and a "hand-dance with the devil" that he was fortunate enough to survive. He writes for the "nomads and misfits," offering his calligraphy as a form of "medicine" for the weary.

To my old friend and colleague: you have always been an architect of words. In *A Stained-Glass Window*, you have built a sanctuary. It is a reminder to us all that it is never too late to manifest the "manna from above" and to finally, boldly, "think big".

Welcome to the world of a writer who has finally decided to "kick down the doors".

—Ambre James-Brown, Head of Global Media, Novo Nordisk A/S, Copenhagen, Denmark and Former Editor-in-chief, The Meter, Tennessee State University, 1997-1999

TABLE OF CONTENTS

Part I
Violence

Genesis 6:11

Now the earth was corrupt in God's sight and was full of violence. (The Holy Bible, NIV)

PUMPKIN

Not only so, but we also glory in our sufferings, because we know that suffering produces perseverance; perseverance, character; and character, hope.

The social worker knocked on the charming, arched door, not knowing what to expect.

She just knew that she was there to investigate abuse and neglect.

The baby's gray, wrinkled grandmother opened the door, and in her arms was a tiny baby girl.

The fragile, delicate little tot was tucked and cradled tightly in a blanket, keeping her warm from the cold air.

Grandma immediately started crying and became visibly upset.

She said, "I hate my son and his girlfriend.

They broke my grandbaby's neck.

Them junkies put bruises all over her body.

Not only that—

She was suffering from malnutrition.

My little Pumpkin was starving."

Grandma opened up the blanket, and the little girl's eyes were sparkling.

Pumpkin could not move her head; she was thin, underweight.

Eight months old.

The social worker started to feel nauseous.

Grandma gathered her composure and said Pumpkin would make a full recovery.

The concerned social worker collected information and took pictures of the house to determine the baby's safety and well-being.

Grandma was fighting for full custody.

The child's parents went to jail, as they should.

This happened six years ago.

Do you think Pumpkin is fully healed?

She probably never will.

By the way,

This is not a fairy tale.

Life gets very real.

Ask Pumpkin.

POTHOLES

Matthew 10:28

Do not be afraid of those who kill the body but cannot kill the soul. Rather, be afraid of the One who can destroy both soul and body in hell.

Juvenile detention centers are filled with young kids caught up in the system, who could have been President Obama or Oprah Winfrey.

Instead, they are losing their sanity behind bars, thinking the same-skinned young man across the tier is their enemy.

How can we change the narrative when deep-rooted generational pain is the catalyst?

The Bible says, "Train a child in the way he should go, and when he is old, he will not depart from it."

This is a gem from Proverbs.

However, all Trey knows is violence because when he was seven, he witnessed his father get shot in the head and bleed out on the curb, next to a pothole.

God forgive these lost souls. For they know not what they do. For they do what they have seen.

Motherless mothers mothering daughters feeling loved less. The only thought in Gabriella's young mind was to have a baby to love because she lived in a hailstorm, and to her, getting knocked up by an older man was the epitome of success.

He was ten years her senior, yet she was a junior in high school. He convinced her to move out of her mother's house and drop out, but she wanted to at least attend night school.

He agreed with reservations, but told her to be cautious and to not make any guy friends.

But she did anyway. On one bitterly cold evening, she was standing in front of the school talking about an assignment when Gabriella's young eyes went wide.

She knew things were about to get violent because her older rapist's car came to a screeching halt, and everything went silent.

He hopped out of the car, smirked, and did not say a word. He just cocked back, pulled the trigger, and left Gabriella bleeding on the curb, next to a pothole.

God forgive these lost souls. For they know not what they do. For they do what they have seen.

NOMAD

Hebrews 11: 8-9

By faith Abraham, when called to go to a place he would later receive as his inheritance, obeyed and went, even though he did not know where he was going. By faith he made his home in the promised land like a stranger in a foreign country; he lived in tents, as did Isaac and Jacob, who were heirs with him of the same promise.

When you see me walking, just know that I am casually passing through.

Hopefully, I greeted you with politeness and the highest of gratitude.

Nothing lasts forever, maybe the sun, stars, and moon.

I have been aiming for those altitudes since exiting my mother's womb.

Please do not take my departure as a falter.

"Oh Father, Thou art in heaven."

The pits of life can feel so bottomless when you are authoring life's experiences.

Devastating losses can by far outweigh exhilarating wins.

The hesitation that ensnares me will be the beginning of my end.

When you see me walking, just know that I am casually passing through.

Hopefully, I greeted you with politeness and the highest of gratitude.

Profusely distance myself from contention.

The growing consensus reveals that God's chosen people have risen.

If you would only listen, you would hear the spirit giving insight into the slightest of whispers.

This is not the Diary of the Wimpy.

Moreso, David versus Goliath victory.

I have read so much irony in the Bible, such as Jesus's crucifixion.

He was mocked because he was weak and could not save himself.

But on the other hand, he showed strength and exonerated mankind from all sin, shame, and guilt.

When you see me walking, just know that I am casually passing through.

Hopefully, I greeted you with politeness and the highest of gratitude.

For I am just a servant, who am I to judge, criticize?

With that being said, I am not perfect.

Looking at my past, how can I scrutinize?

This is the question that I ask myself when I find fault in others.

At the end of the day, we all have struggles, troubles, and muddy rubbish among us.

The thunder and blunders of life can be so troubling at night.

When the regrets of one's consciousness intercept all the nonsense.

Then you wake up in the morning, get dressed, and manifest that you came, saw, and conquered the toxicants of a big ego, pride, or lack of confidence.

When you see me walking, just know that I am casually passing through.

Hopefully, I greeted you with politeness and the highest of gratitude.

A STAINED-GLASS WINDOW

Psalm 84: 1-2

How lovely is your dwelling place, Lord Almighty!
My soul yearns, even faints, for the courts of the Lord; my
heart and my flesh cry out for the living God.

Holy Rosary was the neighborhood Catholic School that I attended as a kid. Although I was not Catholic, it allowed me to get an education outside of what was offered in public schools. At the same time every day, I, along with my classmates, walked around to the church that was connected to the school and prayed to the statue of the Virgin Mary, the mother of Jesus. There was also a designated time for us to go into the sanctuary for mass, where we sang hymns, listened to a homily, and prayed.

The inside of the church was full of breathtaking architecture and symbolic designs. The beautifully colored stained-glass windows were my favorite. They depicted artwork of the life of Jesus Christ, biblical stories, and the connection between heaven and earth. While many church denominations have stained glass artwork, there are some that are very specific to the Catholic faith. For instance, the Sacred Heart of Jesus Christ is Christian art that represents the divine love Jesus has for humanity. It depicts a picture of Jesus that shows his heart being pierced by a lance, surrounded by a crown of thorns, and radiating flames.

In the church, there were also stained-glass windows that depicted the life of the Virgin Mary and various saints. One of the more popular windows is called *The Annunciation*, which depicts the announcement by the angel Gabriel to Mary that she would become the mother of Jesus. *The Pietà*, which is Italian for pity, is a stained-glass window that shows Mary cradling the dead body of Jesus. The original art sculpture was created by Michelangelo Buonarroti and represents the "Sixth Sorrow" of the Virgin Mary.

As a child, I never paid much attention to the fine details of the depictions on the beautifully stained windows. However, I was always astonished by the allure of the colored images. For me, they are grandeur and historic art that will live forever. The Old Testament, Jesus Christ, The Virgin Mary, and so many other components of Christianity are embedded in the sacred illustrations. The windows have been around for a long time, as they date back as far as the seventh century.

Stained-glass windows intrigue me because they tell the story of my favorite book in the world, The Bible. Over the years, it has inspired, elevated, and also humbled me. More than anything, it has made me realize that we are all broken people with an opportunity for redemption. Some of the most well-known figures in the scriptures were flawed, sinned, and made poor decisions. However, it was through the grace of God that their wrongs were forgiven. This is also true for you. The more you read the Bible, the more you will grow and realize that we are all stained-glass windows.

HONESTLY SPEAKING

Ephesians 1:7

In him we have redemption through his blood, the forgiveness of our trespasses, according to the riches of his grace.

In the chill of the night and the haze of the day, I can see your face.

Feel your grace and embrace the mercy that only someone as powerful as you can offer a sinner like me.

It is a wonder that I don't have twenty felonies trailing me.

At times, I feel like life is failing me.

Then I remember how, when I was a kid, you had me winning spelling bees—In, like, the second grade,

Standing up on stages, battling, and winning against kids twice my age.

Then all of a sudden, things started changing

When my parents split.

Now I need a weapon when I walk to school.

I have to keep goons off me, come home, and the electricity is disconnected—

Sitting in darkness, talking

To myself.

"I gotta make it up out of this hellhole, so maybe I need to rub elbows with those that live by the street code and shoot, not free throws,"

But for the stars.

So, I began to run the streets like stray cats.

Stray bullets will make any man lie flat on his stomach,

Close his eyes, and pray that the gunner stops gunning.

Violence was bad for business;

It made the money stop coming.

For real.

I have never condoned killing; it's senseless.

I dodged death by inches.

Seeing my friends in caskets made me want to do better,

Advance to new levels.

Nevertheless, when you are hand-dancing with the devil, it is not that easy to exit.

Believe me.

However, when God has his hands on you, a plan for you, and promised land to you,

He will pull you through like Moses did for them people in bondage.

That's why I pay homage.

Now I educate, meditate, and give thanks to the Most-High God.

At night, I have conversations with him that start at ten and might end at two.

Do it all again the next night.

There is no friend like you,

Yahweh.

SCHOLAR

Colossians 3:23-24

Whatever you do, work at it with all your heart, as working for the Lord, not for human masters, since you know that you will receive an inheritance from the Lord as a reward. It is the Lord Christ you are serving.

I never wanted to be like anybody once I got to college.

It is probably why I skipped a lot of classes.

I just didn't have passion.

The university was a safe haven for me.

Before that, it was the corner:

Gun shots,

Call the coroner,

Police chases,

Dope fiends swarming,

Paraphernalia.

Dorm's boring.

Molded showers.

Financial aid is like a Band-Aid because my student loans
are soaring.

I am paying that money back—

Extortion.

My wage,

Feels minimum.

Retire,

Then you are dead.

Abortion.

I want to be alive,

To enjoy

My portion.

I'm just expressing

My torture.

Average.

Three-time college graduate.

Weirdo.

Norbit.

VIOLATION

2 Samuel 13:14

But he refused to listen to her, and since he was stronger than she, he raped her.

Casey is a twenty-two-year-old white female who has been an alcoholic since the tender age of thirteen.

She later turned to using heroin, which caused her to lose her two young kids to the system.

The Department of Family and Children Services, to be exact.

Her six-year-old daughter was adopted, and her two-year-old son lives with a temporary foster family.

Casey has been in and out of the hospital because of suicidal tendencies.

She believes death is the remedy, but is too afraid to really end things.

As soon as she gets out of the hospital, she goes right back to the track.

Turning tricks to get hits and shoot dope in her discolored veins.

Puncture wounds scar her body.

Opioids destroy her psyche.

But nothing hurts more than the fact that she can't even see her toddler.

She knows that she is selfish.

Addiction has her feeling helpless.

Her family won't even take her phone calls.

However, what I haven't told y'all is that Casey was sexually abused when she was young.

That was the start of her downfall.

You may think that she is a bad person, but she has had bad things happen to her.

Things you would not even imagine.

An eight-year-old girl who was raped by her own daddy.

Sadly.

It is true.

MARGARETTA AVENUE

Matthew 5:21

*"You have heard that it was said to the people long ago,
'You shall not murder, and anyone who murders will be
subject to judgment.'*

Man down.

Don't stand around.

The white sheet—

Too long.

Whoever did it:

Rap Sheet?

Probably not.

Two-tone,

Because black-on-black crime

Suggests we hate our own

People.

Displeased, displaced hate.

The bullet penetrated his cerebrum.

The killer,

Inebriated,

Easily escaped it.

But really,

Did he?

Fifteen years old

And cold-blooded.

Thuggin',

Rugged.

No one ever really loved him

Anyway.

NEIGHBORHOOD

Proverbs 31:8-9

Speak up for those who cannot speak for themselves, for the rights of all who are destitute. Speak up and judge fairly; defend the rights of the poor and needy.

Street names are tagged on walls to honor those who fell to mayhem.

Abandoned buildings become habitats for dope fiends, who smoke dreams and invoke themes of lost hope.

You would think that we were not in America, because all of the store owners are either Asian or Arabic.

Behind bulletproof glasses, taking orders from descendants of dark-skinned Africans.

They may talk with accents, but all firearms utter the same desires and stutter the same language:

It is either rapid—duh duh duh duh duh duh duh duh—

Or endless—bang bang bang bang bang bang bang bang.

Anguish and dark clouds hover.

Disparity isn't subtle.

Why else would we travel an hour to get a decent education?

Despite all this, residents love their neighborhoods, even though the government does not love them.

If schools are public, why should one be greater than the other?

Education may be free, not appropriate, but let's keep that private.

The truth is all tied to the reason why the rich and the poor are divided.

It may not be until the Second Coming that those in power see the greater good.

Until then, this is the reality of inner-city neighborhoods.

HALLELUJAH

Ephesians 5:8

"For you were once darkness, but now you are light in the Lord. Live as children of light."

It is a critical time in my life.

It feels like I am going under.

I see tunnels of darkness—

They haunt me.

There are lives to save.

I hope God anoints me.

I know that I can

Rise up.

Perform miracles.

Jesus is my healer.

My thoughts are mostly spiritual.

How can I avoid death?

I grew up around drug dealers.

My neighborhood bred a lot of killers.

I have mourned at cemetery plots and funerals.

Confessions of a perplexed life.

Robert Frost—

Two roads.

Choose one.

Boom! Guns!

Run!

Hallelujah! Hallelujah!

CHAIN OF EVENTS

Ecclesiastes 3:2

A time to be born and a time to die. A time to plant and a time to uproot.

Guy meets girl.

Girl meets reality.

Guy gets girl pregnant.

They begin to feel gravity.

Girl cannot fathom being young and expectant.

She wants an abortion,

But guy will not let her dead it.

Time goes by, and she has not told her parents.

Only her best friend knows—

She is ashamed and embarrassed.

Teachers at school begin to notice that she is changing.

She has mood swings, sleeps, is gaining weight, and cranky.

Guy is the captain of the basketball team.

He told his mother, and she told him that a baby would destroy his dreams.

One day girl went home, and her parents were waiting at the door.

Mommy gave her a hug;

Daddy called her a whore.

Girl said she was sorry and tried to give her daddy love,

But he pushed her away and said,

"You are not my blood."

She ran to her room.

Mommy followed behind.

Daddy screamed out,

"Have you lost your mind?"

Meanwhile, guy is warming up for a big game on the schedule.

By halftime, he had a double-double.

Division One hoops was inevitable.

The second half was unfortunate—

A totally different story.

He fell and tore his ACL.

And he had just scored forty.

Months went by, and the pressure was building.

Girl became depressed about the thought of having to raise children.

Guy felt despondent because he let his family down.

He started drug dealing.

Girl tried to convince him to stop and focus on his recovery,

But he was making two grand every week,

And hanging out where the thugs be.

Months later, the girl's water broke, and her parents took her in for delivery.

At the same time, guy was on the west side of town on a block that he shouldn't be.

Girl called his phone and excitedly told him the news.

He said that he was on his way, and he would be there soon.

He arrived just in time, but his heart was torn.

Girl died while giving birth, and the baby was stillborn.

How sad.

THERAPY

Psalm 147:3

He heals the brokenhearted and binds up their wounds.

My client is displaying some defiant behaviors at home and school.

Like what?

He is lying, being disrespectful, and feeling angry. Not following the rules. He is in constant conflict with his aunt and siblings.

What's the problem?

Their mother is in prison. She was violent, loved belittling, and hit them.

Sadly enough, both of his brothers also have disabilities.

She deserves to be in jail.

Yeah. Life is not fair. Dayvon has a lot of potential, but he doesn't use the coping skills like deep breathing, meditation, positive visualization, and journaling that were given to him.

How would that help him?

He has been traumatized. Those would help him manage his stress, emotions, and difficult situations effectively. They would turn his weaknesses into strengths. The psychiatrist prescribed him mood stabilizers because he gets really depressed. He has thoughts about death, harming others, and himself.

Poor baby. I know his aunt is worn out. How is she dealing with all of this?

Well, she is doing her best, tired, and having problems with her health. Last month, the doctors told her that she had cancer in her chest, and it had spread to her bones and organs.

Has she told the kids yet?

Nope?

Where will they live if she dies?

Probably in an orphanage. Their family dynamic is damaged. There is no support from others.

That sucks. I wish that we could help them. They will probably be separated and barely see one another. You know that I was raised in foster care, and foster parents don't care.

I remember one time, I ran away because this lady threatened to cut off all my hair. I was just a little girl when her fifteen-year-old son got into bed with me. He didn't do anything, though. I immediately started screaming.

I know that you had a rough childhood, and these kids do, too. I hear stories like this every day, so it's almost like I am immune to them. I don't even know why I am sharing this with you. I shouldn't because of HIPAA laws. I try not to get too involved. Clients like this make me question it all.

Well. You know that you can talk to me about anything. What do you mean? What are you questioning?

If I am really making a difference. I really just sit there and listen. I try to equip him with skills that can help reduce his symptoms and enable him to make better decisions. But the bottom line is, he doesn't seem to be listening.

So now you are blaming the victim?

That's not what I am saying or doing.

Then, stop doing it. That little boy is just a kid. He probably can't even help what he is doing. I'm sure he doesn't feel loved.

He doesn't.

I wish that I could hug him. I feel like crying hearing this.

Don't.

I don't know how you do it. I couldn't do it.

What?

Be a therapist.

SCARS

Isaiah 53:5

But he was pierced for our transgressions, he was crushed for our iniquities; the punishment that brought us peace was on him, and by his wounds we are healed.

Most scars are mental,

Reminders of lessons that were not coincidental.

Bruises build character in losers;

Blemishes breed resilience in winners.

How could something that hurt so bad feel so good when you cross the finish?

Miles and marathons.

In life, there are billionaires and vagabonds.

However, they bleed the same blood and

Deteriorate in the same soil,

Feel the flames of the same furnace.

This goes for the wealthy and the deprived.

In reality, we are dwelling in temporary housing.

Residences are not permanent, but subsidiaries of God's work.

Fingers fiend for murder scenes from the remote control.

Trauma will leave you mute like buttons on a phone.

Anniversaries come and go, but love lasts forever.

Dopamine is touch-and-go until the hugs settle.

Meet-and-greets on social sites end up on Investigation Discovery.

Trick-or-treat on dating sites solicits a predator's felony.

Sorrow soothes the soul of some.

What does it do for you?

It is a fact that tomorrow may never come.

Woo! Hallelujah!

WINS AND LOSSES

I have fought the good fight, I have finished the race, I have kept the faith.

Every good thing must come to an end.

Even though victory feels good, it is not always a win.

If that is the case, what is the purpose of the game being played?

"For what shall it profit a man if he shall gain the whole world and lose his own soul?" is what I am saying

The early bird got the worm, but then it died from a collision.

All species must face the consequences of living.

Neighbors slaughter their family members in the suburbs.

Gangsters drive by, shoot, and water the grass with your blood.

Sick thoughts but true stories.

No guts, then no glory.

Ceddy lost mortgage money at the casino.

Wendy caught her husband sleeping with a cheapo.

 Granny got robbed while leaving bingo.

However, she had a gun in her fanny pack.

Shot the man in his upper back.

Lit up a cigarette and took a puff.

Looked to the sky and said, "What the…."

Bozos in this world love harming kids.

They should all be thrown in prison with broken arms and legs.

Roll them around in wheelchairs and give them cold stares.

Their only meals should be corroded pig ears and old bread.

Politicians are full of waste in a colostomy bag.

They win elections, but the people lose hope in a democracy that fails.

Part II
The Awakening

Ephesians 5:14

Wake up, sleeper, rise from the dead, and Christ will shine on you.

PICTURE THE VOLITION

Hebrews 11:1

Now faith is confidence in what we hope for and assurance about what we do not see.

Have you ever had too much of nothing?

Well, certainly it can be worthy of something.

Delve into the depths of what is not at your fingertips.

Tread in massive oceans.

Hunt in the treachery of jungles.

Your nourishment is not fueled by digestible nutrition.

If people do not *ha-ha* at your vision,

Then your dreams are timid.

Be more than high-level physics.

Let the brainstorm expand your wingspan.

Be majestic.

Ascend like albatrosses and glide,

For you have been called.

Therefore, it is your sworn civic duty

to be uncommon, over average.

Make all the naysayers giggle

When you loose-lip your blueprint.

Remember, you are the architect.

Escort your know-how to the forefront.

Wouldn't you rather have nothing over the fear of never trying something?

ANOMIE

John 8:32

*Then you will know the truth, and the truth will
set you free.*

The Gateway to the West is the city where he was born-St. Louis.

He skipped town to the Grizzlies at nineteen when he was on the run-Memphis.

Started writing with the Titans at twenty-one-Nashville.

Lived with the Terrapins and Capitals to keep his family as one-Maryland and DC

Now he is sleeping with the Bulldogs by his bed-Georgia.

Colossal thoughts of what is possible.

Pocket watchers should be proud of you.

Methodical doubters that doubted you and didn't believe in foresight are diabolical.

Who ever thought that the kid who went from wearing hand me down clothes from Amvets and eating salmon croquettes would gross and invest more than most can project.

He started with a quarter then he got a dollar.

But once he got his hands on a twenty then he wanted thousands.

He had that at sixteen from the triple beam.

Million-dollar dreams and rubber band wads of cash bulging out of Levi's jeans.

Dirty money filled the shoe box listening to Tupac. Do you wanna ride or die playing on the boom box?

Colossal thoughts of what is possible.

Hustle outweighs obstacles.

Obstacles aim is to stop you.

But stopping isn't an option.

He is motivated by moguls,

Whose focus solely is global.

Ghosting the status quo that controls you.

Meeting quotas and thinking of quotables are how his day goes.

Built a downloadable app called Bible Verse Academy but not with Legos.

Download it and see just how your day goes.

Wake up the angels wearing halos that have been protecting you from what is fatal.

He has been scheming since prenatal.

Dreaming even in his crib and cradle.

He had a plan and was able to put food on the table.

Anomie should be his label, come and join, get on the payroll.

A CHIMNEY MOMENT

Galatians 6:9

Let us not become weary in doing good, for at the proper time we will reap a harvest if we do not give up.

Snowstorms warm me like fur coats, and heated, gold glaciers that are in the vicinity.

When I gaze through frost-bitten, foggy, awning windows, I see duplicated images of myself.

But what do you see?

Does your reflection reflect the human being that you once sought to be?

I have not arrived at my destination,

Yet my thoughts breed miracles and manifestations.

The fireside soothes my aging soul.

Adorations of the eradicating sound of logs aflame and pyrography crackling.

At times, the perplexity of my existence causes friction and leaves me wondering what is really happening.

As the amber wood burns in the fireplace. I bow my head and go into a safe space of tranquility.

Ever since Carla was a toddler, she loved dancing, fashion, and modeling.

Her mother was from the motherland, while her father was an islander.

Carla lived a well-balanced life as she thrived in ballet, academics, and drama.

So, naturally, she gravitated to fine arts when she went off to college.

Parties and failed auditions began to cloud Carla's intuition and ambitions.

She soon turned to prescriptions and became addicted to feeling drifted.

All the chemicals in her system conflicted with her inhibitions.

An eighteen-year-old was found dead in the kitchen from an intravenous on Christmas.

Though they were at her fingertips, dreams can seem so distant.

As the amber wood burns in the fireplace. I bow my head and go into a safe space of tranquility.

Often misunderstood

Seeing kids in orphanages and dodging coffins can alter one's thought process.

All I ever wanted was success.

Then I matured and succumbed to the fact that there is no such thing as success.

It is all relative—

Like a family member or a friend who told you that they would be there with you until the end.

Can you hear the vulnerability within?

Hopefully, you can.

I am just venting in quicksand.

Notepads and a pen suffice as my therapist.

Calligraphy is my therapy.

Nomads and misfits are my audience.

Written rhetoric is my medicine.

As the amber wood burns in the fireplace. I bow my head and go into a safe space of tranquility.

PARALLELISM

Ecclesiastes 3:1

*There is a time for everything, and a season for every
activity under the heavens:*

Birds fly south in the wintertime.

Bears break hibernation when it is dinner time.

New Yorkers flee the Big Apple for economic gain.

Is it because of Adam and Eve that we feel pain?

Southerners escaped the master's reign and left the cotton
fields.

Indians settled in the Midwest and left a Trail of Tears.

Time zones change, but not the narratives.

The dark, deep deeds of America are where the devil lives.

Rodney King and George Floyd themes bring molotovs.

Nazis burned the bodies of Jewish victims during the
Holocaust.

Amid the Great Depression, workers got laid off.

In Waco, Texas, David Koresh led a cult, and folks were brainwashed.

Life is a mystery for some, but history depicts the future.

Alex Haley cultivated Roots, and showed you what they did to Kunta.

Birds fly south in the wintertime.

Bears break hibernation when it is dinner time.

New Yorkers flee the Big Apple for economic gain.

Is it because of Adam and Eve that we feel pain?

Tomorrow isn't promised, nor is another minute.

Clocks tick within their internal mechanism.

There are 24 hours in a day, what will you do with yours?

Will you keep knocking for what is promised, or kick down doors?

Greed breeds jealousy and confrontation.

Degrees and spelling bees concoct this occupation.

Quiet nights and caffeine will cause a brainstorm.

Life will have you swinging from tree to tree just to hang on.

The pastor in the pulpit wipes his sweat with a handkerchief.

God's message to the world should relieve anxiousness.

Martin Luther took his last breath in Memphis.

Malcolm got shot in front of his wife and children.

It was a catastrophe when the planes brought down those buildings.

Birds fly south in the wintertime.
Bears break hibernation when it is dinner time.
New Yorkers flee the Big Apple for economic gain.
Is it because of Adam and Eve that we feel pain?

GOLD MEDALLIONS

Luke 4:18

*"The Spirit of the Lord is on me, because he has anointed
me to proclaim good news to the poor. He has sent me to
proclaim freedom for the prisoners and recovery of sight
for the blind, to set the oppressed free,*

Blinded for so long.

Held captive by wicked inhumans,

Who wanted to be sperm donors

And get their crops tended for free.

Trees stand so tall.

Legs dangle.

Heads tangle in nooses—

Tight.

Breathe, young man.

Breathe, my sister.

Flatline, eyes water.

They just killed Ida's daughter.

She got tired of being raped,

And tried to escape during the night.

Generational genocide.

Martin tried.

Malcolm tried.

Black Panther, Black Panther.

The enemy usually comes in disguise:

Smiling face, handshake—

Deep down inside,

Really wants to steal your pride, your dignity.

It worked when drugs inundated black communities in abundance,

Guns booming through the night like an old Negro spiritual.

Schemes to kill dreams.

Ethnic conflict depleted social structures.

Two hundred years later,

And we think we have overcome the struggle.

Big rings on knuckles.

Vehicles that are luxury.

High fashion, the result of not having.

Thick gold chains wrap around necks

In memory of master.

The first shall be last in life after

Death.

VAGABOND

Proverbs 19:17

Whoever is kind to the poor lends to the Lord, and he will reward them for what they have done.

You have a place to lay your head

What are you complaining about?

When it is raining, pouring, frozen, or cold?

You don't dwell under a bridge, bus stop, vacant lots, shelters, abandoned buildings, man-made tents, or park benches.

You don't dig through trash bins, beg pedestrians, starve, refrain, forgo, or have hunger pains.

The world doesn't ignore your mental health—depression, post-traumatic stress disorder, schizophrenia, anxiety, bipolar disorder— that you can't get treated because you do not have health insurance benefits.

You are not at high risk for infectious, non-infectious diseases: viral hepatitis, tuberculosis, human immunodeficiency virus, diabetes, heart disease, or lung disease.

For future reference, the next time you see a person who is homeless, you don't have to approach them, but you can encourage, pray, not judge, donate, acknowledge that had it not been for God's grace, mercy, blessings, love, and kindness, then this could be you.

Down and out.

Destitute.

LANDMARK

You are at the intersection of many streets in all states and municipalities.

Witnessed so many casualties and fatalities that did not have to be.

People stand on you, waiting for Ubers, Lyfts, buses, and taxis.

Little kids jump up and down on you.

In huge metropolises like New York City, you are chaotic, iconic.

For some, you are a crossroad to the hustle and bustle,

The turning point to the dividends that ensnare us all.

The angle at which you are positioned allows us to view life from many standpoints.

At night, you are lonely, quiet, staring at the adjacent.

It is the illumination from the streetlights that enhances your visibility.

In inner cities, you are a commodity.

You bring out the worst in society.

Drug deals and overdoses.

Riots and atrocities.

The Corner.

TENNESSEE STATE UNIVERSITY

Proverbs 18:15

The heart of the discerning acquires knowledge, for the ears of the wise seek it out.

Beautiful shades of melanin encompass me, like

Dark brown, light brown, slight yellow, light yellow.

Intellectual minds of curious teens pursuing higher education,

Chasing their dreams.

Sororities strolling through the congested courtyard, so sophisticated and debonair,

Hair swinging, hips flinging.

Fraternities stepping and hoofing in sequence, clapping and chanting to the rhythms ricocheting through the air.

The atmosphere is so inspiring and inviting, enticing adulterous inclinations of insubordination.

Don't be late for class because the professors wear afros, pump fists, marched with the Big Six, and were a part of the movement of the advancement of colored folk.

They will tell you that college is not a party, party, party.

It is a privilege, privilege, privilege.

Do you know how many negroes died and sacrificed their lives

For you to make a mockery of and not be in your seat when class begins?

Look to your left, look to your right—

One of your friends will not be here when it is time to graduate.

Better learn to balance, navigate, think straight, and make wise decisions.

I did not comprehend this back then,

Still trapped in the snare, unaware, ill-prepared for an HBCU:

Tennessee State University,

Better known as TSU—

Go Big Blue!

It would be remiss of me if I didn't mention the world-famous Aristocrat of Bands:

Musical excellence, precision, Grammy Award winners, with a rich tradition.

Much respect.

THINK BIG

Matthew 17:20

He replied, "Because you have so little faith. Truly I tell you, if you have faith as small as a mustard seed, you can say to this mountain, 'Move from here to there,' and it will move. Nothing will be impossible for you."

What is the point of

Living

If you don't have a

Vision?

A road map is like wheels with

Intention,

Steering,

Gearing,

You to a preplanned destination.

For you,

You only.

Money is

Temporary.

Who takes it to the

Cemetery,

Where buried dreams lie beneath the soil of

Devastation?

Are you

Worried yet

That your purpose will never surface,

Like the dust that settles in

Caskets?

You can still salvage the

Carnage,

But that's only

If you want it.

Do you want it?

Do you have it?

Don't dismiss it.

Enlist it.

Inhale it.

Drink it.

It's liquid.

How sacred,

Greatness,

Bold,

Bodacious,

Is Vision

MINISTER

James 4:6

***But he gives us more grace. That is why Scripture says:
God opposes the proud but shows favor to the humble.***

Arrogance and pride have been the downfall of many.

Do not let it be yours,

For it was once mine.

Egos are powerful.

Evil is plentiful.

Indecency is pervasive.

The world can be so hateful.

Do you choose to indulge in the forsaken?

Let love be your haven.

Wealth lies in what is sacred.

Eyes are similar to a soliloquy;

They speak volumes and hold memories.

Silence silences friends and enemies evenly.

Water under the bridge is the epitome of forgiveness.

I have negligently offended many in my lifetime, and if you are one of them, then forgive me.

Just as you have been forgiven.

The Cross.

A LOVE TALE

Ecclesiastes 4: 9-12

Two are better than one, because they have a good return for their labor: If either of them falls down, one can help the other up. But pity anyone who falls and has no one to help them up. Also, if two lie down together, they will keep warm. But how can one keep warm alone?

Crisis.

Catastrophe.

I feel lifeless.

Calamity.

Emergency.

Our baby needs diapers.

Disaster.

Gusts of wind.

Hurricane.

No windshield wipers.

Close your eyelids.

The light bill is due.

Darkness.

 Blackout.

Night.

Obscurity.

Lightlessness.

We need groceries.

Edibles.

Perishables.

Eggs and noodles.

Vegetables.

I wish we could have sex, but all this stress is unbearable.

Oppressive.

A bit much.

Unacceptable.

We hardly even communicate—

Converse,

Speak,

Chat,

Talk.

Pressure.

Lack of finances—

Capital,

Currency,

Assets—

 Is tearing us apart.

Baby, we will be okay.

We will get ahead of this economy.

Unethical.

Underhanded.

Illegal.

Corrupt.

Skeptical.

As long as we stay together,

We will get through whatever:

Anything,

 Everything,

Far and few,

In between.

Please do not leave,

I love you.

THE BETTER HALF

Luke 7:37-38

A woman in that town who lived a sinful life learned that Jesus was eating at the Pharisee's house, so she came there with an alabaster jar of perfume.

As the curves bend and lanes switch,

Continue to spiral upward, my dear.

The travel jerks uphill;

Torrents of maltreatment misguide your discernment.

See-saw, ill-advised connections—

You adore the teetering.

Downgrades consume the headway that is behind you.

May I ask,

When will the anticipation of poignancy cease?

Values should align at the intersection of curiosity.

Boundaries emerge from the depths of courage.

Never underestimate the value of contentment.

Discover the abyss dialogue that fuels the clandestine.

Concepts the dearth esteem that hinders your essence.

You are divine.

Consider being chaste for once.

Preserve your alluring anatomy.

Pandora's Box.

GENTLE DAMSEL

Luke 7:47

Therefore, I tell you, her many sins have been forgiven—as her great love has shown. But whoever has been forgiven little loves little.

They had another argument.

She could tell he had been drinking again.

He tried to kiss her, but she told him that he reeked of a Scottish sailor from all the whiskey on his breath.

Not to mention his lips were coated with another woman's crimson lipstick.

She hastily turned her head when he leaned in.

He asked what her problem was and if she still loved him.

He always gets emotional when he has had too much to drink .

She told him that he needed to lie down, and they would continue the conversation tomorrow.

He combatively snatched her arm.

When he doesn't get the response that he likes, he gets violent.

He grabbed her face with his thumb and three of his fingers.

Then he squeezed her cheeks together, tight, causing her lips to protrude.

As you can imagine, he smothered her lips with his and swirled his tongue down her throat.

After he was done, she hawked a big gob of spit up his nostrils.

He smacked her, and she fell back against the stove.

He walked towards her with a sinister smirk on his face.

That's when she reached onto the counter and grabbed a knife from the block.

Without hesitation, she leaned into his pot belly, and the blade pierced through layers of tissue.

Paralyzed, he looked down at her, eyes wide, and mouth ajar.

He reached for his stomach, where the blood profusely poured out of him.

He fell to his knees.

She turned her back to him, patiently retrieved her phone, telephoned the police, and waited.

Forgive me, I am not sorry to hear that he did not make it.

Do I need to put my hands behind my back so you can put the cuffs on?

If not, I'm going on the porch to smoke a cigarette.

MEMORIAL DAY

Luke 2 34-35

Then Simeon blessed them and said to Mary, his mother:
"This child is destined to cause the falling and rising
of many in Israel, and to be a sign that will be spoken
against, so that the thoughts of many hearts will be
revealed. And a sword will pierce your own soul too."

You do not have to be the smartest.

Keep your chin up.

Hold your head high.

You look very nice in your corduroy pants.

I was not sure if that Izod sweater would fit your thin frame.

There was also a nice pair of penny loafers that I was going to buy for you at Goodwill,

But your feet are getting so long—

You would not be able to wiggle your lengthy toes into them.

I want you to remember to use your manners today:

Please, thank you, yes ma'am, no ma'am.

And smile.

Don't have your face all fixed to be unkind.

Here is your lunch box. I packed your favorite treat.

A burned bologna sandwich smeared with mayonnaise and chocolate chip cookies that I baked last night.

I also got you a bag of those jalapeno potato chips that you like.

It is a bit frigid today, so I want you to wear your voluminous bubble coat.

Come here, baby. Hug Mommy before you go. Mommy loves you.

Bye.

Thirteen years ago, I watched you walk out the door, not knowing that it would be the last time that I stared into your face.

I will never forget the smell of the charred meat that I prepared for you that morning.

Today, it is the anniversary of the day that you walked out of the house and never returned.

I will always remember you.

Thank you for the conversation.

KENYATTA

1 Thessalonians 5: 16-18

Rejoice evermore. Pray without ceasing. In every thing give thanks: for this is the will of God in Christ Jesus concerning you.

I hate my job. I wish that I had not woken up this morning.

These types of thoughts can rob you of the true joy and happiness that God has meant for you.

Have you ever been to a hospital and witnessed the pain of a dying cancer patient?

Better yet, how do you think kids bedridden in hospitals feel?

Terrible, right?

However, they would probably do anything in their power to have the ability to wake up in good health.

If you can get out of bed, move all your limbs, and roam freely, then you are blessed.

Don't take the little things for granted.

Kenyatta is seven years old and has brain cancer.

She has been in and out of the hospital her entire life.

Chemotherapy caused her hair to bald, and she has dark bags under her eyes.

If I took you to the hospital to meet her, she would greet you with a big, beautiful smile.

She learned the lesson of not letting anything, or anyone, steal her joy.

If Kenyatta can do it, then why can't you?

She was just seven years old and died this past June.

Be thankful….

Part III
Redemption

Psalm 111:9

He provided redemption for his people; he ordained his covenant forever— holy and awesome is his name.

SPIRIT OF DAVID

Psalm 23:1-6

A Psalm of David. The Lord is my shepherd; I shall not want. He makes me lie down in green pastures. He leads me beside still waters. He restores my soul. He leads me in paths of righteousness for his name's sake. Even though I walk through the valley of the shadow of death, I will fear no evil, for you are with me; your rod and your staff, they comfort me. You prepare a table before me in the presence of my enemies; you anoint my head with oil; my cup overflows....

I don't know why you care for me so much,

Or why you are there for me, preparing me for what is to come.

I have all this education, which feels like mitigation, negotiations.

There are so many stipulations when you have a background such as mine.

Thought process.

Climb.

Friends doing time.

With family, there is a thin line,

Which infringes on my sanity.

But with you, it's different.

You make me feel like I'm special.

Gifted.

Humble vanity.

See, you sought me, then I sought you.

Life fought me, then I fought you.

So many angles are obtuse, acute.

I am hardly ever right-handed.

I guess that is why I have vindictive, afflicted, adult temper tantrums,

When problems come in threes—random tandems.

Dancing on my deep, thought-provoking insomnia nights.

Fight, flight, plights

You say it is going to be all right, all right.

All right, you are right.

Why do you care so much?

It is only by grace, mercy, and prayer that I am the man that I have become,

My God.

HOLY, HOLY, HOLY

Revelation 19:11

I saw heaven standing open and there before me was a white horse, whose rider is called Faithful and True. With justice he judges and wages war.

I am thinking:

Do or die.

Gazing up at the pale blue sky,

White clouds amidst.

Irritation embodies closed fists.

Poverty-stricken elements and incidents.

Premonitions of barbed-wire fences.

Courtrooms with prosecutors.

Boardrooms with mobster figures.

Engulfed in realism.

Cornered in capitalism.

Explore the righteous baptism.

Holy, Holy, Holy

Survived corners with double crosses.

Collided with street bosses.

Arrived, thrived, multiple markets.

Success, the ultimate target.

His eyes are on the sparrow

Sleep, King of Egypt, Pharaoh.

You have to be careful

Of whom you put up on a pedestal.

Jesus rode in on a white horse.

He rose from the corpse.

Showed up, of course.

Just my chosen thoughts.

Holy, Holy, Holy

Paid debts to society.

No such thing as equality.

Owe the fiends an apology.

Blasphemy is a mockery.

Only God can bless me.

Paul the Apostle was special to me.

He instilled hope after the treachery.

Punished and persecuted the Jewish,

Christians and those who pursued it.

Disciple Judas was foolish,

Like when Brutus killed Julius.

It was Moses who freed Israel.

Abraham fathered Ishmael.

Jesus met a woman at a still well;

He gave her salvation.

But the Romans said:

"Murder, Murder!

Kill Him!"

Holy Holy Holy

AMBIENCE

Psalm 119:165

Great peace have those who love your law, and nothing can make them stumble.

Marshmallows at the bonfire.

Sopranos sing in the church choir.

Sweet silhouettes are projected by the sunset.

Narcos and ammunition land on private jets.

Handshakes from fake friends can feel condescending,

But so can pancakes when you don't add the syrup.

Ketamine manages pain and causes hallucinations.

Amphetamines are stimulants that will have your thoughts racing.

Shallow, heated water fills the hot tub.

Oily hands from Japan caress back rubs.

Cheap shots from the opposition get no response.

Only Godly talk can serenade in my ambience.

Pinot Noir fine wine swirls in the stemware.

Monologues and dialogues appear from out of thin air.

Hairs flare unkempt out of gray beards.

Stem cells propel and differentiate these ideas.

Touchscreen fingerprints smear the kiosks.

Technology is replacing all the teens' jobs.

Screen time, social media can leave you blind and senile.

She thought it was true love, but it was just a rebound.

Can you see now?

SPLASH

Genesis 2:15

The Lord God took the man and put him in the Garden of Eden to work it and take care of it.

I started earning money for myself at a very young age.

It was at an upscale car cleaning service, Elite Detailing, located in the Central West End neighborhood of St. Louis, where I made my first dollar.

It felt so good, and it was rewarding to see a vehicle come in dirty and leave looking like new.

At the time, I was thirteen, maybe fourteen years old.

My friend's uncle briefly played in the NFL and opened the car wash after moving back to the city.

The summer heat in "The Lou" is sultry,

But flinging water all over my face and onto the luxury vehicles kept me cool most of the time.

The winters were the total opposite.

St. Louis is for sure in the Midwest, and it gets bone-chilling frigid.

In that climate, the water is almost frozen, and that was not pleasant for my fingers.

Hold on. I believe that I mentioned luxury cars.

Yes. I did. Elite Detailing was not your ordinary run-of-the-mill car wash.

We shampooed the interior of vehicles, waxed, and buffed the highest of high-end makes and models.

When I was still a kid, I drove Porsches, Benzes, BMWs, Saabs, Alpha Romeros, Volvos, Cadillacs, Range Rovers, and the list goes on....

Thus, comes my love for luxury cars.

The doctors, lawyers, businessmen, and other professionals who could afford those vehicles really inspired me to dream big.

They instilled very expensive aspirations in me.

Not to mention, the owner of the shop ingrained in me an unyielding work ethic that I continue to possess.

I used to sit in the lobby area of the shop and read the newspaper before we opened.

One day, the owner looked over at me and said, "You are going to be somebody one day."

I looked up at him and then ducked my head back down into the daily sports news section of the St. Louis Post-Dispatch.

The words that he spoke to me did not resonate until years later.

I always try to speak positively into the lives of those whom I encounter.

Words of encouragement can change the trajectory of someone's day or life.

In closing, cars are only needed to get from point A to point B.

Their value depreciates as soon as the papers to finance them are signed.

However, despite the car you drive, do your best to keep it tidy.

Despite the job you may have, make sure you are thankful for it and do it well.

My first job was cleaning cars.

What was yours?

A WRITER'S ANXIETY

Philippians 4:6

Do not be anxious about anything, but in everything by prayer and supplication with thanksgiving let your requests be made known to God.

I am still trying to break up with the old me.

Ancient sentiments, familiar dispositions that ambush the war zone in my mind.

Deception drags me into these disastrous downward spirals that snag me.

Dreams die, fall by the wayside;

Ashes of false hope spread across the seaside.

The fear of being irrelevant saturates my brainwashed denials.

I, too, can be Pulitzer Prize-winning is the opening of my benediction.

The beginning of my consecration commences.

I am distancing myself from repeated ambiguity, apprehension, reluctance, and skepticism.

I am tired of making a mess of my preposterous pessimism.

I just want to be what God has destined.

Manifest the manna from above and under-the-table blessings.

Plagiarism is an unacceptable weapon.

Don't be deceived by the deception.

He intentionally made you special.

But you have to believe that you are.

YOUNG ARTIST

1 Timothy 4:12

Don't let anyone look down on you because you are young,
but set an example for the believers in speech, in conduct,
in love, in faith and in purity.

Your craft is a weapon, so use it to be a change agent.

Never waver, be open-minded.

Journey deep into your creative abilities so that no one can say you are a replica.

Though, analyze those who achieved greatness before you—

There is nothing new under the sun.

Shine a million times bright.

Be certain that even when the curtains close, you will still be under surveillance.

Patrons will undoubtedly criticize, scrutinize.

Due diligence does not supersede the commentary.

Vigilance will not calm the downpour, rhetoric.

Venture into the hailstorm and take on the hysteria of being novel.

Spotlights project imagination, creation—

Creativity, visualization, or original thought processes.

Be subjectively subjective.

It is okay.

You are an artist.

That is the objective.

ART CARPE DIEM

Exodus 35:35

He has filled them with skill to do all kinds of work as engravers, designers, embroiderers in blue, purple and scarlet yarn and fine linen, and weavers—all of them skilled workers and designers.

Paintings soothe the imagination.

Dancing is good for the soul.

Music makes you feel like you have someone that you can relate to.

Films are entertaining.

Sculpting is captivating.

Literature is meaningful and allows one to express their human experience through words.

Architecture is fascinating.

Have you ever painted on a canvas and made a beautiful mess?

When was the last time you moved your body to the rhythm of music?

How often do you binge-watch your favorite TV show on a lazy Saturday?

Did you know that your favorite coffee mug was probably sculpted out of clay?

What is the last book that you read that caused you to reflect and discern its meaning?

Have you ever considered the level of skill required to design and construct a massive skyscraper?

Jean-Michael Basquiat was a groundbreaking Neo-Expressionist painter known for his primitive style of painting.

Misty Copeland was the first African American woman to be a principal dancer with the American Ballet Theater.

Stevie Wonder is a singer, record producer, and songwriter who is one of the most influential musicians of the twentieth century.

Spike Lee attended a Historically Black College University and is a renowned filmmaker who explores race relations, urban issues, and political themes (Do The Right Thing).

Meta Vaux Warrick Fuller was a female artist who used the sculpting art form to celebrate the Black Experience during the Harlem Renaissance.

Maya Angelou was an award-winning author and poet who tackled themes of identity, racism, and resilience. She was brilliant.

Paul Revere Williams was a pioneering African American architect known for designing over three-thousand structures, including the Los Angeles County Courthouse.

Without art, imagine life… imagine life without art…

HORN OF AFRICA

Proverbs 31:30

Charm is deceptive, and beauty is fleeting; but a woman who fears the Lord is to be praised.

It felt like a high school dance when I saw you clapping your hands and shaking your hips. So carefree.

I held my camera in amazement, thinking…..

Who is this?

Click. Click. Click. Click. Click. Click. Click.

Snapshot after snapshot

Your curves caught my attention. The way you smiled and danced on rhythm captivated me.

I was thinking. I know she will be my wife someday, though I never believed in love at first sight.

I gently put my camera down to my side as you casually approached me.

Hey. You do not have my permission. Why are you taking photos of me? She said, giggling.

Hi. My name is Justin. You are ridiculously photogenic. I hope you are having a great time. I get paid to capture moments. I am just doing my job.

Okay. Cool. But I would appreciate it if you would not post me on the internet, Instagram or Facebook. It is against my religion.

Yeah sure. I apologize. No worries. Since you asked nicely, I won't do that. By the way, where are you from? You have a distinct accent.

I'm from Ethiopia. It's located in the Horn of Africa. East Africa, to be exact. We are surrounded by Eritrea, Djibouti, Somalia, and Kenya.

Africa huh. From the moment that I saw you, I knew that you were different. You are beautiful. Do you think we could….

Go out and have a drink. Grab a bite to eat. Blah Blah Blah. I have heard all of that before. No thanks.

Well, I was thinking more like…the African American museum, then smoothies, maybe a food truck if you get hungry. I want to learn more about your background.

You should get back to your job now; she said, grinning and blushing. If you want to continue this conversation, then meet me tomorrow at 7. I will be on the corner of 13th and U Street. There's no need for my number.

My name is Mahi.

JUBILEE

It is a day of celebration,

Good food and great times.

Everyone has been waiting for this occasion for weeks.

Uncle Billy has been grilling since five o'clock this morning—

Ribs, chicken, burgers, brisket, and of course, those juicy red-hot links.

Aunt Cassie knows she can make a mean, cheesy macaroni.

I can't wait to dig my fork into those gooey, creamy noodles.

She will probably bake her award-winning pineapple and coconut cakes, too.

My beautiful Aunt Johnetta sure does whip up a tasty potato salad.

Everybody doesn't know how to mix those potatoes with mustard, mayo, eggs, and whatever else she puts in there.

Now, a cookout isn't a cookout if you don't have baked beans. Aunt Dee Dee, let me tell you. She makes the best summertime barbecue beans that your mouth has ever tasted.

My Uncle Greg is going to bring the "packaged liquor." A party is not a party without adult beverages. He always makes sure everyone has a good time.

The reality is that I will never see these aunts and uncles again because they are no longer physically here with us. But, in my outlandish imagination, we just had an amazing family reunion.

HALF OF A CENTURY

2 Corinthians 4:16

Therefore we do not lose heart. Though outwardly we are
wasting away, yet inwardly we are being renewed
day by day.

Bald spots appear from either aging or pulling of hair.
Back pains emerge from lifting out of a chair.
Once your eyesight diminishes, your vision is impaired.
Bones lose density, and tendons tend to tear.

Fifty Years of Living
Nothing really surprises you anymore.
You are wiser and so mature.
No obstacle is impossible.
Even the hospital is like a tour.

Fifty Years of Living
You do not take small gestures for granted.
The questions of life will never be answered.
First, the biopsy, then the cancer.

Family urns upon the mantle.

Fifty Years of Living

Pacemakers regulate the rhythm of the heart.

Paydays come around once or twice a month.

Segues into heydays are yet to come.

Migraines and headaches permeate through the skull.

Fifty Years of Living

Social media is a gift and a curse.

Insecurities leech, and they lurk.

Social Security cannot be treated by a nurse.

Disease-free bells ring throughout the church.

Fifty Years of Living

Night lights warm the chilled room.

Grandbabies howl in the full moon.

Libations always brighten the dull mood.

Fugazi telepathy transmits a fool's jewels.

Fifty Years of Living

You are not ready to wave the white flag.

Exercise delays the jet lag.

Filet mignon comes wrapped in doggy bags.

Palladium plates stacked with salad and succotash.

Fifty Years of Living

MATURATION

Hebrews 5:12-14

In fact, though by this time you ought to be teachers, you need someone to teach you the elementary truths of God's word all over again. You need milk, not solid food! 13 Anyone who lives on milk, being still an infant, is not acquainted with the teaching about righteousness. 14 But solid food is for the mature, who by constant use have trained themselves to distinguish good from evil.

For we do not choose our beginning;

That was the choice of our parents and Creator.

We just wail when we are delivered,

Shivering from the chill.

Then we nap,

Swallow milk to satisfy our craving.

Ga-ga and goo-goo.

Digest baby food.

First, there is crawling, then steps are taken.

No more jibber and jabber.

It is more like the terrible two—

Three, four, five.

Now you are off to school, kindergarten.

The basics, foundation, and all the fundamentals that have cultivated your brain.

In middle school, you just want to fit in, and everybody is strange.

High school is a far cry from anything you have ever experienced.

Decisions weigh heavily as graduation draws near.

So much fear and anxiety:

What will I do with my life?

Should I get a job or go to college?

I will lose my best friend.

This is so unfair.

Time has passed, and it's time to marry.

You have settled into your career.

Once a baby, and now you have babies.

Do not spoil the grandbabies.

You retire, fall ill, and fight for a few years.

Physically, you have become invisible,

But your spirit is enduring.

Were you well-behaved enough to get into the place called paradise?

Did you accept the Lord as your Savior?

That is between you and your God.

Life.

GRAY HAIRS

Proverbs 20:29

The glory of young men is their strength, gray hair the splendor of the old.

The elders are all dying, fading.

No more family reunions, get-togethers.

Therefore, where is the guidance, leadership?

Blind leading the blinded

The Bible says, "Seek and ye will findeth."

What are we seeking at this age?

Peace, love, security, and kindness.

Almost fifty years young, balancing life's cycles.

Juggling jaded perspectives, politicians, and hypocritical objectives.

One day, our lives will be like a museum, complete with distant memories.

No more instant gratification.

That was the younger me.

Now it is easier to resist the temptation.

My mood swings in motion, unpredictable emotions.

Anxiety about health issues triggers thoughts about wills, trust funds, and my adult children.

My wife:

Will she be at my bedside and hear my dying words?

Or will I be sobbing, crying, listening to hers?

Perturbed in my reflection of the middle-aged experience,

Adjusting to the gray hairs, reading glasses, and life's turbulence.

It is not over until the casket has closed,

Or the ashes burn.

Cherish the mid-life chaos.

You only live once.

LAST WORDS

Revelation 20:6

Blessed and holy are those who share in the first resurrection. The second death has no power over them, but they will be priests of God and of Christ and will reign with him for a thousand years.

I know that one day I will transition, go and meet my God. Deathbeds are unavoidable, like lawyers, obstacles, and alibis.

No matter how many garments are in my closets and cars are in my garages,

I am still going to get that call for my troubled soul, bones, and double entendres.

If I should die today, ask the mortician to calmly fix my face with a smile.

I overcame the odds.

Monopolies always astonished me, but there is nothing more precious than living godly.

Yahweh groomed me for this moment, initiated my atonement,

Told me to fear no opponent.

The man in the mirror is the only opponent.

If my hair is nappy, don't comb it.

Just comb through my journals, then burn them.

My words are already eternal.

So is my journey as a journalist.

All I ever wanted to be is a writer. It fulfills my desires. Me and my thoughts in the quiet of the night.

Please don't condemn me for my sins. Honesty mirrors a lens. Me and my thoughts in the quiet of the night.

My life is stained, unhinged, and unchained.

For many years, I felt deranged.

Edgar Allen Poe authored my pain

Asylums for my father, Vietnam, insane.

At a loss for words, I cannot explain.

Have you ever hit a fleeing deer in the headlights and felt shame?

This poet is forever losing balance on this derailed, smoke-filled, turned-over train,

Called life.

But do not feel sorry for me.

Meet me at the tabernacle.

Go to the altar for me.

Bow your head.

Say a prayer.

Monologues, allegories.

All I ever wanted to be is a writer. It fulfills my desires. Me and my thoughts in the quiet of the night.

Please don't condemn me for my sins. Honesty mirrors a lens. Me and my thoughts in the quiet of the night.